Mr. Bell's ⭐ TOP HAT

Written by Sally Prue

Illustrated by Liz Catchpole

Rigby

Mr. Bell has a big top hat

that

pops

up

tall

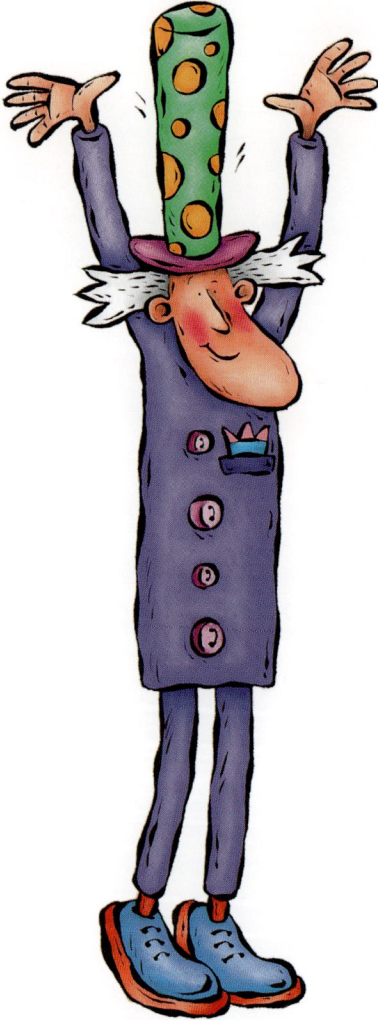

or squashes **flat**.

Here's a boat for Mr. Bell.

Here's a tray for tea as well.

When Miss Mot
got very hot,
it cooled her down
an awful lot.

Here's a nest for a hen to sit.
Here's a snug and comfy fit.

A bed for a pet,

a fishing net.

Even a place
for gelatin to set.

Here's a bucket for
a clown.

Here's a bag to take
to town.

Fancy that!
A fancy hat!
Oh what a hat,
that does all that!